ULTIMATE MACHINES

Tanks and Military Vehicles

Rob Colson

PowerKiDS
press™

New York

Published in 2013 by The Rosen Publishing Group, Inc.
29 East 21st Street, New York, NY 10010

Senior Editor: Julia Adams
Produced by Tall Tree Ltd
Editor, Tall Tree: Jon Richards
Designer: Ed Simkins

Library of Congress Cataloging-in-Publication Data

Colson, Rob.
 Tanks and military vehicles / by Rob Colson.
     p. cm. — (Ultimate machines)
 Includes index.
 ISBN 978-1-4777-0067-9 (library binding) — ISBN 978-1-4777-0119-5 (pbk.) —
 ISBN 978-1-4777-0120-1 (6-pack)
 1. Tanks (Military science)—Juvenile literature. 2. Vehicles, Military—Juvenile literature. I. Title.
 UG446.5.C58 2013
 623.74'7—dc23
                              2012021180

Manufactured in the United States of America

CPSIA Compliance Information: Batch #W13PK6: For Further Information contact Rosen Publishing, New York, New York at 1-800-237-9932

Contents

War Machines

Motorized vehicles play a major part in warfare. Armored vehicles carry guns, soldiers, or equipment onto the battlefield.

Tanks are heavily armored, have tracked wheels for traveling over rough areas, and are usually armed with a large gun on a rotating turret. Other armored vehicles carry troops or help with building work.

Amazing design

Tanks and many other military vehicles use tracks. This means that a band of linked plates covers the wheels. Tracks spread the weight of the vehicle across a wide area. This stops it from sinking into soft ground.

Early tanks

Tanks were developed during World War I. The British used their first tank, the Mark I, in the Battle of the Somme in 1916. The Mark I was able to cross enemy trenches. It was a great success and more models quickly followed. Germany responded to the new threat by developing special antitank guns.

Early tanks such as this British Mark IV from 1917 did not have a main gun on a turret. Instead, guns were fitted to either side of the tank.

A Chinese Type 99 tank fires its main gun. The most advanced tank in the Chinese army, the Type 99 has a powerful 125 mm gun and a top speed of 50 miles per hour (80 km/h).

Panzer Tanks

The name "Panzer" comes from the German word for "armor." It was the name given to German tanks during World War II.

Germany developed many new Panzers during the war, including the Tiger I, a fearsome tank with strong armor and a powerful gun.

The Tiger I was too heavy to cross small bridges, so it was designed to move through water up to 13 feet (4 m) deep. This allowed it to cross most rivers.

TECHNICAL DATA

Tiger 1
YEARS OF SERVICE
1942–1945
ENGINE **Gas**
NUMBER OF CYLINDERS **12**
ARMOR **1–4.7 inches (25–120 mm)**
MAIN GUN **88 mm**
TOP SPEED **24 miles per hour (38 km/h)**
WEIGHT **62.7 tons (56.9 t)**
CREW **5**
RANGE **121 miles (195 km)**

Big gun

The Tiger I was designed in 1942 to replace the smaller Panzer IV. The Panzer IV did not have a big enough gun to destroy Soviet T-34 tanks, even at close range. The Tiger I was armed with an 88 mm gun that fired huge rounds and could destroy an enemy tank from up to 2.5 miles (4 km) away. However, it was expensive to produce, and fewer than 1,400 were built. By comparison, the Soviets built 35,000 T-34s.

An American soldier poses on top of an overturned Tiger I in Normandy, France in 1944. Germany had too few tanks to stop the larger Allied forces.

Amazing design

The Jagdpanzer 38 was a tank destroyer, which is a light tank designed to attack other tanks. It had sloped armor at the front and back. This was designed to deflect enemy shells, causing them to bounce off the armor rather than pierce it.

M4 Sherman

The M4 Sherman tank was built by the United States during World War II, and used by US and British forces.

The Sherman was reliable and easy to maintain, which gave it an advantage over the powerful but less reliable German tanks.

US troops advance through a Belgian town under cover of an M4 Sherman in September 1944. Nearly 50,000 Shermans took part in World War II.

Strength in numbers

The Sherman was a medium-weight tank with thin armor. It had a much less powerful main gun than the German Tiger 1 tank. The front armor of a Tiger was very strong, so the Shermans had to fire on them from the side or the back to damage them. A Tiger could destroy a Sherman from any angle. However, the Shermans won many battles with German tanks by fighting in very large numbers.

The gunner sat on a seat just beneath the turret so that his head was at gun-height.

Amazing design

The Sherman was the first US tank to have a fully rotating gun turret. The turret was fitted with a device called a gyrostabilizer. This kept the gun steady as the tank crossed bumpy ground, allowing the gunner to aim the gun accurately.

TECHNICAL DATA

M4 Sherman
YEARS OF SERVICE
1942–1955
ENGINE **Gas**
NUMBER OF CYLINDERS **12**
ARMOR **2 inches (53 mm) at front;
2.5 inches (63 mm) at side; 1.6 inches
(40 mm) at back**
MAIN GUN **75 mm**
TOP SPEED **30 miles per hour (48 km/h)**
WEIGHT **33 tons (30 t)**
CREW **5**
RANGE **120 miles (193 km)**

Challenger 2

The Challenger 2 is a main battle tank built for the British army. Main battle tanks (MBTs) are large tanks that play an important role in modern armies, supporting infantry (soldiers on foot) in battle.

The Challenger 2 is one of the most advanced MBTs in the world. Its powerful main gun has a range of more than 5 miles (8 km).

A Challenger 2 is protected by a special material called Chobham armor. This is a ceramic that is twice as hard as any metal.

TECHNICAL DATA

Challenger 2
YEARS OF SERVICE **1998–present**
ENGINE **Diesel**
NUMBER OF CYLINDERS **12**
ARMOR **Chobham armor**
MAIN GUN **120 mm**
TOP SPEED **35 miles per hour (56 km/h)**
WEIGHT **69 tons (62.5 t)**
CREW **4**
RANGE **280 miles (450 km)**

Tank crew

The Challenger 2 has a four-person crew. The commander is in charge of the tank. The loader operates the radio, loads the gun, and prepares food for the rest of the crew. The driver steers the tank and looks after the engine. The gunner controls the turret and fires the gun. The crew can see outside the tank by looking through periscopes. Each crew member is trained to do all four tasks in case one of them is injured.

The commander of a Challenger tank keeps watch through a periscope. The gunner sits in front of him, controlling the turret.

Amazing design

To find its way around at night, the Challenger 2 is fitted with a night vision sensor in its turret. Night vision either detects heat instead of light or it boosts the small amount of light it detects to create a picture like the one above.

T-72

The T-72 is a Russian main battle tank. It is a very light tank that can cross small bridges that heavier enemy tanks cannot cross.

To keep the tank as small as possible, the crew of the T-72 works in very cramped conditions. There is so little space inside the tank that the crew members all have to be no more than 5 feet 3 inches (1.6 m) tall.

Amazing design

Many T-72s are fitted with a special type of armor called reactive armor. This is made of special bricks that are fitted to the outside of the tank. The bricks explode when a weapon such as a missile hits them. This explosion destroys the missile before it can get through into the interior of the tank and kill the crew.

An Iraqi T-72 fires its main gun during the Iraq War. Originally made for the Soviet Union and its allies, the T-72 is now used by armies all across the world.

Although it is a small tank, the T-72 is fitted with a very large 125 mm gun. As well as firing at the enemy, the gun barrel can smash through concrete walls up to 16 inches (40 cm) thick.

Laser rangefinder

The T-72's gun is fitted with a laser rangefinder. The rangefinder shines a powerful beam of laser light at the tank's target and measures the time it takes for the beam to be reflected back. The time taken tells the crew how far away the target is.

TECHNICAL DATA

T-72

YEARS OF SERVICE
1973–present
ENGINE **Diesel**
NUMBER OF CYLINDERS **12**
ARMOR **Steel and composite**
MAIN GUN **125 mm**
TOP SPEED **30 miles per hour (48 km/h)**
WEIGHT **46 tons (41.5 t)**
CREW **3**
RANGE **286 miles (460 km)**

APCs

Armored personnel carriers (APCs) are designed to carry troops to the battlefield. They are known to soldiers as "Battle Buses."

APCs vary widely in design. Some are lightly armored to protect against small weapons. Others have two layers of heavy armor to protect against powerful explosives. APCs are also fitted with weapons such as machine guns and grenade launchers.

Amazing design

Many APCs are amphibious. This means that they can travel on land and through water. Amphibious APCs are used to carry troops to the shore during an attack from the sea. They are carried close to the shore by special warships called amphibious assault ships.

Ukrainian APCs land on a beach during a training exercise. They power through the water using propellers, just like boats.

Light APC

The M113 (right) is the most widely used APC in the world. It was first developed in the 1960s by the US Army as a vehicle that could be carried into combat zones by plane. Its armor is made from the light metal aluminum. This makes it strong enough to protect its crew from most small weapons fire, but still light enough to be carried by plane.

An M113 finds shelter in a launderette in Panama City during a US operation in Central America. It is small enough to go where larger tanks cannot go.

TECHNICAL DATA

M113
YEARS OF SERVICE **1960–present**
ENGINE **Diesel**
NUMBER OF CYLINDERS **6**
ARMOR **1.5 inches (38 mm) aluminum**
MAIN GUN **M2 Browning machine gun**
TOP SPEED **30 miles per hour (48 km/h)**
WEIGHT **13.5 tons (12.3 t)**
CREW **2 plus 11 passengers**
RANGE **300 miles (480 km)**

Engineering Vehicles

Military engineering vehicles carry out building work in combat zones. This includes digging trenches or knocking down obstacles.

The vehicles may be diggers, bulldozers, cranes, or backhoes—all the vehicles that you find on a building site. They can also be fitted with tools that are only found on the battlefield, such as mine-clearing rakes.

Amazing design

The M728 is an American engineering vehicle. The ones shown above have been fitted with mine-clearing rakes. The rakes lift mines buried in the soil and push them to the side without exploding them. This clears a path wide enough for tanks and other vehicles to follow safely.

Armed engineer

This M728 engineering vehicle is used in demolition (knocking down buildings). It is fitted with a winch for lifting and carrying and a bulldozer blade for pushing over walls. The M728 is also heavily armed, carrying a 165 mm main gun that can be used to blast holes into walls.

The Pionierpanzer Dachs is a German engineering vehicle that is based on the Leopard 1 tank. In place of the main gun, it is fitted with a digging bucket.

TECHNICAL DATA

M728

YEARS OF PRODUCTION
1965–1987
ENGINE **Twin-turbo diesel**
NUMBER OF CYLINDERS **12**
ARMOR **5.6 inches (143 mm)**
MAIN GUN **165 mm M135**
TOP SPEED **30 miles per hour (48 km/h)**
WEIGHT **55 tons (50 t)**
CREW **4**
RANGE **280 miles (450 km)**
CRANE CAPACITY **9 tons (8 t)**

AVLBs

Armored vehicle-launched bridges (AVLBs) are combat support vehicles that carry metal bridges.

AVLBs allow tanks and other armored vehicles to cross rivers. They are needed where there are no other bridges nearby, or where existing bridges are too narrow or too weak to support the weight of heavy armored vehicles.

Some AVLBs are converted trucks. The chassis (frame) of the truck needs to be very strong to support the weight of the bridge, which can weigh more than 16.5 tons (15 t).

TECHNICAL DATA

M60

YEARS OF SERVICE **1987–present**
ENGINE **Diesel**
NUMBER OF CYLINDERS **12**
GEARBOX **2-speed**
RANGE **288 miles (464 km)**
TOP SPEED **30 miles per hour (48 km/h)**
CROSS COUNTRY SPEED **7.5–11 miles per hour (12–18 km/h)**
WEIGHT **56 tons (51 t)**
CREW **2**
BRIDGE LENGTH **62 feet (19 m)**

Converted tank

The M60 (pictured right) is an AVLB used by the US Army. Its main body is similar to the body of a tank, with tracked wheels to allow it to travel over rough land carrying the bridge on top. The bridge is folded while it is not being used. This kind of folded bridge is called a scissor bridge. When unfolded, the scissor bridge can cover a river that is up to 60 feet (18 m) wide. It can hold a weight of up to 77 tons (70 t), strong enough for most kinds of armored vehicles.

Amazing design

An M60 can make a bridge in less than five minutes. Once the bridge has been unfolded and laid in place, the AVLB detaches itself from the bridge and moves aside to allow the tanks and other vehicles to cross. The AVLB is the last to cross. it reattaches itself to the bridge once it is on the other side, and the bridge is folded back into place.

Robot Wars

Some military vehicles are unmanned robots operated by remote control. Robot vehicles are sent to places that are too dangerous or too small to send people.

Robot vehicles have been developed to operate on land, in the air, and underwater. Today, most robot vehicles are small and light, but in the future, even large tanks may be unmanned.

TECHNICAL DATA

Ripshaw

YEARS OF PRODUCTION
2009–present

ENGINE SIZE **Diesel**

SUSPENSION TRAVEL
16 inches (400 mm)

ARMOR **Unarmed**

TOP SPEED **more than 62 miles per hour (100 km/h)**

WEIGHT **8,820 pounds (4,000 kg)**

PAYLOAD CAPACITY
1,984 pounds (900 kg)

HEIGHT **6 feet (1.8 m)**

The Ripshaw is an experimental unmanned light tank. It is designed to be fast and flexible. The Ripshaw is not well armored, but its light frame allows it to accelerate to 50 miles per hour (80 km/h) in just 3.5 seconds.

Amazing design

Unmanned aerial vehicles (UAVs) are used today mostly for reconnaissance missions. This means that they are sent over enemy territory to gather information about enemy positions. In the future, fighter jets will be unmanned. Their human crew will control them safely from the ground using satellite links.

The MQ-1 Predator is a UAV in the US Air Force. It can fly up to 460 miles (740 km) to a target, and remain overhead for 14 hours gathering information before returning to base.

Cameras on this SUGV's head allow its operators to see exactly where it is going.

Small robots

Small unmanned ground vehicles (SUGVs) are light and small enough to be picked up by hand. They are used in military operations in cities, where they can be sent into tunnels, sewers, or pipes. SUGVs are controlled using systems originally designed for game consoles.

Glossary

accelerate (ik-SEH-luh-rayt) To increase in speed.

amphibious (am-FIH-bee-us) A vehicle that can travel on both land and water.

armor (AR-mer) A coating of metal or other strong material that protects tanks from gunfire.

barrel (BAR-ul) Part of a gun. The barrel is a long, thin metal tube through which a bullet is fired.

bulldozer (BUL-doh-zer) A machine used in construction to push large amounts of soil, sand, or rubble from one place to another.

ceramic (suh-RA-mik) A material such as clay that is made very hard by heating it, then allowing it to cool.

cylinder (SIH-len-der) A chamber in an engine inside which pistons pump up and down.

machine gun muh-SHEEN GUHN) A gun that fires many rounds of bullets very quickly with one pull of the trigger.

occupation (ah-kyoo-PAY-shun) A period during which one country is ruled by another country that has taken control by military force. During World War II, Germany occupied much of Europe.

periscope (PER-uh-skohp) A thin tube with mirrors in it that sticks out at the top of a tank. It allows the crew to see where they are going.

propeller (pruh-PEL-er) A kind of screw at the back of a ship that rotates to push the ship forward. Many amphibious armored personnel carriers are fitted with propellers to power them in water.

range (RAYNJ) The distance a vehicle can travel on one tank of fuel. Also used for the distance a gun can fire.

reconnaissance (rih-KAH-nih-zents) A military mission to find out information about the enemy. Reconnaissance involves moving into enemy territory, so it can be extremely dangerous.

round (ROWND) A casing that is loaded into a gun. A round contains gunpowder and a bullet or missile.

turret (TUR-et) A rotating platform on a tank on which the main gun is mounted.

winch (WINCH) A machine used to lift heavy objects. A rope is attached to the object and then wound around a cylinder to lift the object.

Models at a Glance

Model	Years Made	Number Built	Did You Know?
Mark 1	1915–1919	150	While it was being developed, the Mark 1 was called "tank" to hide its true purpose. The name stuck.
Challenger 2	1993–2002	446	To confuse the enemy, the Challenger 2 can create smoke using smoke grenades fitted to its turret.
M4 Sherman	1941–1943	50,000	The US originally planned to build more than 100,000 M4 Shermans, but they ran out of steel.
Tiger 1	1942–1944	1,347	Today there is just one Tiger 1 left in working order. It is kept running by the Tank Museum in Dorset, England.
T-72	1971–present	115,000	The T-72 was designed to be able to cross small bridges in Eastern Europe that larger tanks could not cross.
M113	First made in 1960	80,000	The M113 is partly amphibious. Its tracks power it through the water.
M728	1965–1987	291	The main gun of the M728 has a short barrel. It fires high explosives during demolition operations.

Websites

Due to the changing nature of Internet links, PowerKids Press has developed an online list of websites related to the subject of this book. This site is updated regularly. Please use this link to access the list:
www.powerkidslinks.com/ulma/tank/

Index